Atkins Diet Lunch Recipes

Delicious Atkins Diet Recipes for Home or Work for Busy People

Disclaimer

Table of Contents

Introduction

I want to thank you and congratulate you for purchasing the book, *"Atkins Diet Lunch Recipes – Delicious Atkins Diet Recipes for Home or Work For Busy People"*.

This book contains proven steps and strategies on how to prepare easy dishes that are always perfect for lunch.

Many of us are always on the go, especially during the day. Having an extremely hectic schedule both at home and at work is the main reason why most people pay less attention to what they eat during lunch. For people who want to practice the Atkins Diet heartily, preparing foods for lunch should not become a problem anymore.

This book contains plenty of lunch recipes that you can follow so you can prepare healthy and tasty dishes in just a few minutes.

Thanks again for purchasing this book, I hope you enjoy it!

Chapter 1: Atkins Diet Overview

Also called the Atkins Nutritional Approach, the Atkins diet is a diet program that promotes the consumption of less carbohydrate and more of fats and proteins. The diet has become widely embraced by many people because of its effectiveness in weight loss.

The body uses glucose as its main source of energy and it comes from foods that are rich in carbohydrates such as breads, cereals and other starchy fruits and vegetables. If a person consumes high amount of carbohydrates, then his body will store the unused energy into fats. This will eventually lead to weight gain.

According to research, a low-carbohydrate diet will switch the body's metabolism from using glucose as energy over to utilizing the body's stored fat as energy. If the body uses the stored fat as energy, it will eventually lead to weight loss.

However, Atkins diet does not suggest the total elimination of carbohydrates in the diet to shed body fats fast. If you want to try this way of eating, you must follow some steps in order for the diet to be effective without causing any other health issues.

There are four phases in Atkins diet:

Induction phase - This is the most crucial part of the diet because this is when you will introduce your body to a low-carb meals. People who are used to eating foods rich in carbohydrates may find this phase very challenging. This phase will give the body ample time to adjust its metabolism and to convert stored fats to energy.

Total daily consumption of carbohydrates should be 25 grams or less. The phase lasts for about 2 weeks or until you have already lost a significant amount of fats. Acceptable sources of carbohydrates are mostly green leafy vegetables.

Phase 2 - By this time, the body has already gained a momentum in shedding fats. This phase is when you can raise your total intake of carbohydrates to 50 grams. However, it is advisable to raise it in 5-gram increments to give the body time to adjust. You have to be in this phase until you are already within 10 pounds of your goal weight. You can now add some fruits to your carbohydrate sources.

Phase 3 - This is the time when you can fine-tune your diet and find out what works and what does not work for you. You can raise total intake of carbohydrates to 80 grams and you can add more fruits and starchy vegetables in your carbohydrate sources. This lasts for about a month or until you have already reached your desired weight.

Phase 4 - Ideally, you have already reached your goal weight by this time; the importance of this phase is for you to maintain it. You can eat almost all foods that you have been eating prior to dieting, but you still need to watch your daily intake of carbohydrates. At this phase, you can raise your daily carbohydrate intake to 100 grams, but you can make adjustments based on your body's needs.

A carefully planned meal will ensure that you can get all the carbohydrates you need without going overboard. However, sticking to the diet during lunch is a challenge to many diet enthusiasts because of busy work schedules and other circumstances. However, the recipes presented in the next chapters will prove handy in making sure that you can still eat a delicious lunch that adheres to the Atkins diet plan.

Chapter 2: Easy Recipes for Vegetables

Dishes with Vegetables

Spicy Asparagus

Ingredients:

500 grams asparagus

8 bacon slices

4 eggs

3 ribs celery

½ teaspoon dried chili flakes

3 tablespoons fresh lemon juice

2 tablespoons olive oil

1 tablespoon vegetable oil

2 tablespoons fresh tarragon leaves, chopped

Dash of salt

Dash of pepper

Preparation:

- Rinse the asparagus and pat them dry. Trim the woody ends.

- Put 2 cups of water in a pot, season it with salt and pepper and then bring it to a boil.

- When the water boils, put the asparagus into the pot and cook for about 3 minutes. Remove the asparagus and set aside to cool.

- In another pot, put another 2 cups of water, let it boil and then reduce the heat.

- Crack the egg into a bowl and gently slide it in simmering water.

- Let the egg cook for about 3 minutes or until it is opaque white in color.

- Use a slotted spoon to transfer the egg into a plate. Cook the eggs one at a time to avoid overcrowding the pot.

- In a skillet, heat a tablespoon of vegetable oil and then cook the bacon slices for 3 minutes or until crisp.

- Transfer them in paper towels to absorb excess oil. Chop them coarsely and set aside.

- In a bowl, whisk together the lemon juice, olive oil and chili flakes. Season it with salt and pepper.

- In a large plate, combine the asparagus, celery, tarragon and bacon.

- Pour the oil mixture over the asparagus and gently toss to combine.

- Top with poached eggs and serve.

- This makes four servings.

Roasted Mixed Veggie

Ingredients:

2 cups Brussels sprouts

1 large cauliflower

8 slices bacon

2 cloves garlic, minced

¼ cup raisins

2 tablespoons vegetable oil

2 tablespoons olive oil

10 strands saffron

¼ cup pine nuts

Preparation:

- In a skillet, heat vegetable oil and cook the bacon slices for about 3 minutes per side or until crisp.

- Put them in paper towels to absorb excess oil. Chop the bacon coarsely and then set aside.

- Put the pine nuts in a baking tray and roast in the oven at 375 °F for about 5 minutes or until golden brown. Set aside to cool.

- Put a cup of water in a pan and add the raisins to it.

- Bring the water to a boil and let the raisins cook for about 20 minutes; drain the water and let the raisins cool.

- Trim the cauliflower and cut into small florets.

- Trim also the Brussels sprouts and cut them into half.

- In a large bowl, combine cauliflower, Brussels sprouts, garlic and olive oil; season the mixture with salt and pepper.

- Transfer the vegetable mixture in a baking pan lined with aluminum foil.

- Put the baking tray in the oven and roast at 300 °F for about 25 minutes or until tender and slightly caramelized.

- In a large bowl, combine the roasted vegetables, raisins, bacon and pine nuts.

- Season the mixture with salt and pepper and serve.

- This makes 4 servings.

Beet Carpaccio

Ingredients:

8 medium beetroots

4 eggs, boiled

3 tablespoons fresh lemon juice

1 teaspoon lemon zest

1 sweet onion, chopped

2 tablespoons olive oil

2 teaspoons sweetener

2 tablespoons capers, rinsed and drained

3 tablespoons fresh dill, chopped

Dash of salt

Dash of pepper

Preparation:

- Trim the leaves of the beetroots, but leave at least half an inch of the stalks.

- Put the beetroots in a deep pot and cover them with water.

- Bring the water to a boil and then let it simmer. Cook the beetroots for about 40 minutes.

- Drain the water in the pot and let the beetroots cool.

- In a bowl, whisk together the olive oil, lemon juice, lemon zest, capers, onion, dill and sweetener; season the mixture with salt and pepper and set aside.

- Peel the eggs, cut them into halves and set them aside.

- Remove the skins of the beetroot and then trim the top and bottom part.

- Slice the beetroots very thinly and put them in a large bowl.

- Pour the dressing over them and gently toss to combine.

- Serve the beetroots with boiled eggs.

- This makes 4 servings.

Baked Vegetables

Ingredients:

4 medium zucchinis, sliced thinly

4 carrots, diced

2 medium eggplants

3 cloves garlic, sliced thinly

6 medium tomatoes, sliced thinly

2 medium onions, sliced thinly

½ cup tomato paste

1 cup cherry tomatoes

2 tablespoons parsley, chopped

1 tablespoon dried oregano

½ cup olive oil

½ cup feta cheese, crumbled

Preparation:

- Slice the eggplants into rounds with half an inch thickness.

- Heat some olive oil in a pan and fry the eggplant slices for about 5 minutes per side or until golden.

- Transfer the cooked eggplant slices in a large bowl.

- In the same pan, sauté garlic and onion for about 5 minutes or until tender.

- Transfer the sautéed mixture into the bowl with the eggplant.

- Add the tomatoes, carrots, zucchini, tomato paste, oregano, parsley and 1 cup of water to the bowl.

- Gently toss to combine all the ingredients. Season the mixture with salt and pepper.

- Transfer the mixture in a large baking dish and drizzle the remaining olive oil on top.

- Put the baking dish in the oven and bake at 425 °F for about 30 minutes.

- Remove the baking dish from the oven and sprinkle feta cheese on top of the vegetable mixture.

- Put the baking dish back in the oven, reduce the heat to 375 °F and continue to bake for another 20 minutes.

- Let the baked vegetables cool before serving.

- This makes 4 servings.

Stir-fry Veggie

Ingredients:

2 cups cabbage, sliced thinly

½ cup shiitake mushrooms, sliced thinly

½ cup chestnuts, sliced thinly

1 cup snap peas

3 spring onions, sliced thinly

1 clove garlic, minced

1 red onion, sliced thinly

1 red chili, sliced thinly

1 teaspoon sesame oil

2 tablespoons olive oil

2 teaspoons soy sauce

8 slices bacon

1 tablespoon sesame, toasted

Dash of salt

Dash of pepper

Preparation:

- In a skillet, heat 1 tablespoon vegetable oil and fry the bacon slices for about 3 minutes per side or until crisp.

- Transfer the bacon slices on paper towels to absorb excess oil. Let them cool and chop them coarsely.

- In a bowl, combine onions, springs onions, chili and garlic. Set the mixture aside.

- In a separate bowl, combine the snap peas, mushrooms, cabbage, and chestnuts. Set the mixture aside.

- Heat the oil in a wok and then add the onion mixture to it. Stir the mixture for about 2 seconds.

- Add the vegetables mixture and the chopped bacon to the wok and then stir for another 2 minutes.

- Season the mixture with soy sauce and sesame oil.

- Transfer the mixture to a serving dish and sprinkle sesame seeds on top.

- This makes 4 servings.

Braised Cabbage

Ingredients:

4 cups red cabbage, chopped

1 red onion, sliced thinly

½ cup balsamic vinegar

2 apples

1 tablespoon fennel seeds, bashed

2 tablespoons butter

2 tablespoons olive oil

½ cup parsley, chopped

8 slices bacon, chopped

Dash of salt

Dash of pepper

Preparation:

- Peel the apples, remove the cores and cut them into bite-size pieces. Set them aside.

- Remove the outer leaves of the cabbage, cut it into half and remove the core. Chop the cabbage into bite-size chunks and set aside.

- Peel the onion, slice it very thinly and then set aside.

- Heat the olive oil in a pan and cook bacon and fennel seeds until golden.

- Add the onions to the pan and continue to cook until sticky.

- Add the apples, cabbage and vinegar to the pan.

- Season the mixture with salt and pepper and stir well.

- Cover the pan and simmer for about 1 hour. Stir regularly.

- Transfer the dish to a serving bowl and garnish with chopped parsley before serving.

- This makes 4 servings.

Zucchini Noodles

Ingredients:

2 medium zucchinis

1 cup snap peas

1 cup broccoli florets

1 cup cabbage, sliced thinly

2 cloves garlic, minced

4 eggs

3 tablespoons olive oil

3 tablespoons sesame oil

2 tablespoons soy sauce

3 tablespoons white wine vinegar

2 teaspoons ginger, grated

Dash of salt

Dash of pepper

Preparation:

- In a bowl, whisk together the sesame oil, vinegar, soy sauce and ginger.

- Season it with salt and pepper and then set aside.

- Peel the zucchinis and use a spiralizer to cut them into long strips. You can also use a sharp knife to cut them into thin strips.

- Put the zucchini strips in a large bowl and set aside.

- Heat the olive oil in a nonstick pan and fry the eggs one at a time. Set them aside.

- Boil 2 cups of water in a deep pot; add the cabbage, broccoli and snap peas to the pot.

- Let the vegetables cook for about 1 minute or until slightly wilted.

- Drain the water and transfer the vegetables to the bowl with the zucchini strips.

- Pour the dressing over the vegetables and gently toss to combine.

- Top the vegetables with fried eggs and serve.

- This makes 4 servings.

Cheesy Baked Veggie

Ingredients:

2 cups broccoli florets

2 cups cauliflower florets

2 tablespoons butter

2 tablespoons olive oil

2 tablespoons fresh thyme, chopped

2 cloves garlic, minced

2 cups almond flour

¼ cup almond flour

¼ cup almonds, slivered

½ cup cheddar cheese, grated

Preparation:

- Heat the butter in a small pan and sauté the garlic for about 2 minutes.

- Add the almond flour to the butter and stir well until a paste forms.

- Add the almond milk to the paste and whisk until it turns into a smooth mixture.

- Add the broccoli florets to the mixture and let them cook for about 20 minutes.

- Remove the pan from heat and mash the broccoli.

- Add half of the grated cheddar cheese to the mashed broccoli and mix well.

- Lightly brush olive oil on a large baking dish.

- Arrange the cauliflower florets in the baking dish and pour over the mashed broccoli.

- Sprinkle evenly the chopped thyme and almonds on top of the mashed broccoli.

- Top it with the remaining grated cheddar cheese.

- Put the baking dish in the oven and bake at 375 °F for about 1 hour.

- This makes 4 servings.

Roasted Squash Salad

Ingredients:

1 butternut squash

12 slices bacon

2 cups arugula

1 teaspoon coriander seeds

1 teaspoon red chili flakes

4 tablespoons white wine vinegar

1 tablespoon vegetable oil

6 tablespoons olive oil

½ cup Parmesan cheese

Dash of salt

Dash of pepper

Preparation:

- In a skillet, heat 1 tablespoon vegetable oil and cook the bacon slices for about 3 minutes per sides.

- Transfer the bacon on paper towels to absorb excess oil, chop them coarsely and set aside.

- In a bowl, combine salt, pepper, coriander seeds and chili flakes. Set the mixture aside.

- Peel the butternut squash, remove the seeds and cut it into bit-size chunks.

- Put the butternut squash chunks in a baking tray line with aluminum foil.

- Pour olive oil over the butternut squash.

- Sprinkle the chili mixture on the squash and then toss to coat.

- Put the baking tray in the oven and bake at 375 °F for 30 minutes or until golden brown.

- Transfer the butternut squash chunks in a plate and let them cool.

- In a small bowl, whisk together the remaining olive oil and the balsamic vinegar.

- Season it with salt and pepper and drizzle over the butternut squash chunks.

- Sprinkle grated parmesan cheese before serving.

- This makes 4 servings.

Dishes with Vegetables and Egg

Mixed Veggie Fritata

Ingredients:

8 eggs

1 bunch of asparagus

1 carrot

2 cloves garlic, minced

¼ teaspoon cayenne pepper

1 white onion, sliced thinly

3 tablespoons olive oil

½ cup cheddar cheese, shredded

¼ cup Parmesan cheese, grated

3 tablespoons parsley, chopped

Dash of salt

Dash of pepper

Preparation:

- Peel carrot, dice it and then set aside.
- In a bowl, whisk together eggs, parsley, parmesan cheese and cayenne pepper. Season it with salt and pepper.

- In a skillet, heat 1 tablespoon olive oil and add diced carrot to it. Stir and cook for about 5 minutes or until tender.

- Transfer the diced carrot to a plate and set aside.

- Put the remaining olive oil to the pan and sauté onion for about 5 minutes or until soft and tender.

- Add the asparagus to the skillet and continue to cook for another three minutes. Season it with salt and pepper.

- Reduce the heat and add the diced carrot and the egg mixture to the pan.

- Spread the shredded cheddar cheese on top of the egg mixture. Let it set for about 5 minutes.

- Transfer the skillet to the oven and broil for about 3 minutes or until the frittata is golden brown on top.

- Let the frittata cool before slicing.

- Garnish it with chopped parsley and serve.

- This makes 4 servings.

Egg Salad

Ingredients:

12 eggs

8 Boston lettuce leaves

1 tablespoon fresh dill, chopped

1 stalk celery, chopped

1 small red onion, chopped

2 teaspoons fresh lemon juice

2 tablespoons Dijon mustard

½ cup mayonnaise

Dash of salt

Dash of pepper

Preparation:

- Put onion in a bowl and cover with water. Let stand for 10 minutes and then drain the water.

- In a pot, put the eggs and cover with cold water. Cover the pot and bring the water to a boil.

- Cook the eggs for 1 minute and then remove the pot from heat. Let the eggs stand in hot water for 8 minutes and then transfer them in a bowl with cold water.

- Peel the eggs, slice them into bite-size chunks and then set aside.

- In a large bowl, combine celery, onion, mustard, lemon juice and mayonnaise. Season the mixture with salt and pepper.

- Add the eggs to the bowl of mayonnaise and gently toss to combine.

- Lay a lettuce leaf and put some egg mixture on the center.

- Fold the leaf into a wrap. Continue to wrap the remaining ingredients.

- This makes 4 servings.

Egg Meatballs

Ingredients:

8 hard-boiled eggs

250 grams ground pork

½ cup almond flour

2 eggs, beaten

½ cup vegetable oil

½ cup coconut flakes

2 tablespoons cilantro, chopped

¼ cup parsley, chopped

½ teaspoon paprika

2 lemons, wedged

Dash of salt

Dash of pepper

Preparation:

- Peel the eggs and set aside.

- In a bowl, combine ground pork, paprika and cilantro. Season it with salt and pepper.

- Divide the meat mixture into 8 equal portions. Cover the eggs with the meat mixture.

- Dust the meat-covered eggs with some flour, dip them in beaten eggs and dredge them in coconut flakes.

- In a pan, heat the oil and fry the meat-covered eggs for about 5 minutes or until golden brown.

- Transfer the meat-covered eggs in paper towels to absorb excess oil.

- Cut them into halves and garnish with chopped parsley.

- Serve with lemon wedges.

- This makes 4 servings.

Zucchini Fritters

Ingredients:

4 medium zucchinis

¼ cup almond flour

1 egg, beaten

2 tablespoons vegetable oil

2 cloves garlic, minced

2 tablespoons parsley, chopped

Dash of salt

Dash of pepper

Preparation:

- Peel zucchinis and grate them; place grated zucchinis in a bowl, sprinkle a dash of salt and let stand for 8 minutes.

- Place grated zucchinis in paper towels to absorb extra liquid.

- Transfer grated zucchinis in a large bowl.

- Add garlic, egg, Parmesan cheese and almond flour to the bowl. Combine all ingredients.

- Season the mixture with salt and pepper.

- In a pan, heat vegetable oil, scoop a tablespoon of zucchini mixture and fry it for about 2 minutes per side or until golden brown.

- Fry in batches to avoid overcrowding the pan.

- Place the fritters in paper towels to absorb excess oil.

- Sprinkle chopped parsley on fritters before serving.

- This makes 4 servings.

Egg Stir-Fry

Ingredients:

4 eggs, beaten

250 grams shrimp, peeled and deveined

2 cups bean sprouts

1 teaspoon ginger, grated

2 tablespoons parsley, chopped

4 spring onions, chopped

1 tablespoon olive oil

Dash of salt

Dash of pepper

Preparation:

- In a skillet, heat olive oil and stir-fry the shrimps for about 3 minutes or until they turn pink and opaque.

- Add ginger, spring onions and bean sprouts to the pan. Continue to stir-fry for another two minutes.

- Reduce the heat and add the beaten eggs to the pan.

- Allow the beaten eggs to set a little bit and then stir to combine all ingredients.

- Season the mixture with salt and pepper.

- Transfer the mixture in a bowl and top with chopped parsley.

- Serve immediately.

- This makes 4 servings.

Easy Egg Salad

Ingredients:

4 eggs

12 slices bacon

2 cups green beans

1 tablespoon vegetable oil

3 tablespoons olive oil

1 teaspoon yellow mustard

1 tablespoon white vinegar

4 spring onions, chopped

2 cups romaine lettuce, torn into bite-size pieces

Preparation:

- In a bowl, whisk together vinegar, mustard and olive oil. Set aside.

- In a skillet, heat a tablespoon of vegetable oil and cook the bacon for about 3 minutes or until crisp.

- Transfer bacon in paper towels to absorb excess oil.

- Chop the bacon coarsely and set aside.

- Put the eggs in pan, cover them with cold water and then bring it to a boil for about 5 minutes.

- Transfer the eggs in a bowl of cold water; when eggs are cold enough to handle, peel them and cut them into quarters.

- Put the green beans in the pan, cover with cold water and bring it to a boil. Cook for about 3 minutes and then transfer green beans in a bowl of cold water.

- Drain water and transfer the green beans to a large bowl.

- Add the chopped bacon and spring onions to the bowl.

- Pour the dressing over the salad and gently toss to combine.

- Top the salad with eggs and then serve.

- This makes 4 servings.

Chapter 3: Easy Recipes for Red Meat

Dishes with Beef

Steak Guacamole Wrap

Ingredients:

500 grams rib eye steak

1 cup shiitake mushrooms, sliced

2 avocados, peeled and pitted

2 cloves garlic, sliced thinly

2 spring onions, sliced thinly

¼ cup coriander, chopped

2 red tomatoes, halved

½ teaspoon ground cumin

2 tablespoons olive oil

3 tablespoons fresh lime juice

1 tablespoon paprika

1 teaspoon dried oregano

2 tablespoons olive oil

4 tablespoons sour cream

6 butter lettuce leaves

Dash of salt

Dash of pepper

Preparation:

- Put the tomatoes, spring onions, cumin, garlic, coriander and avocados in a food processor and then pulse to a paste.

- Transfer the paste to a bowl and add lime juice and olive oil to it.

- Season it with salt and pepper and then mix well. Set the guacamole aside.

- Heat a griddle pan and sear the mushrooms; set them aside.

- Season the steaks with paprika, oregano, salt and pepper.

- Heat a little olive oil in the griddle pan and cook the steak for about 5 minutes per side.

- Let the steak cool, slice it thinly and then set aside.

- Lay a lettuce leaf on a flat surface and spread some guacamole on it.

- Place some sliced steak, mushrooms, coriander leaves and red chilies on top of the guacamole.

- Top it with some sour cream and then fold the leaf into a wrap.

- Continue to wrap the remaining ingredients.
- This makes 6 servings.

Ground Beef Wrap

Ingredients:

500 grams ground beef

1 cup tomato puree

1 green bell pepper, seeded and diced

1 cup kidney beans, rinsed and drained

1 sweet onion, diced

1 tablespoon sweetener

2 tablespoons red wine vinegar

½ teaspoon chili powder

2 teaspoons Dijon mustard

1 cup radicchio lettuce, sliced thinly

8 lettuce leaves

Dash of salt

Dash of pepper

Preparation:

- Put the ground beef in a pan and cook over medium heat for about 5 minutes or until slightly brown.

- Add the onion and the bell pepper into the pan and continue to cook for another eight minutes.

- Add the tomato puree to the pan and stir to combine.

- Add also the chili powder, mustard, sweetener and vinegar to the pan.

- Add the kidney beans and stir well. Season the mixture with salt and pepper and bring it to a boil.

- Cook until the mixture thickens. Let it cool.

- Lay a lettuce leaf on a flat surface and put some beef mixture on it.

- Top it with sliced radicchio lettuce and fold the leaf into a wrap.

- Continue to wrap the remaining ingredients.

- This makes 4 servings.

Beef Burger

Ingredients:

500 grams ground beef

1 egg

1 cucumber

8 pieces Portobello mushrooms

1 cup lettuce, sliced thinly

4 medium tomatoes

1 teaspoon red chili flakes

2 tablespoons fresh tarragon, chopped

1 small red onion, chopped finely

2 tablespoons vegetable oil

½ teaspoon nutmeg

1 teaspoon Dijon mustard

¼ cup Parmesan cheese

Dash of salt

Dash of pepper

Preparation:

- Brush some olive oil on the Portobello mushrooms and season them with salt and pepper.

- Put them on the grill and cook for about 3 minutes per side.

- Set them aside to cool.

- In a bowl, combine the beef, onion, mustard, tarragon, egg, nutmeg, chili flakes and Parmesan cheese.

- Season the mixture with salt and pepper.

- Form the mixture into four patties and chill them in the refrigerator for about 30 minutes.

- Heat a little vegetable oil in the griddle pan and then cook the burger for about 5 minutes per side.

- Arrange the burger. Use the Portobello mushrooms as buns.

- Combine the cucumbers, lettuce and tomatoes in a bowl.

- In a separate bowl, whisk together 2 tablespoons olive oil and lemon juice. Season it with salt and pepper.

- Pour the dressing over the vegetables and gently toss to combine.

- Serve the burgers with the salad.

- This makes 4 servings.

Grilled Steak Salad

Ingredients:

500 grams flank steak

1 head romaine lettuce, torn into bit-size pieces

4 radishes, sliced into strips

1 avocado, peeled, pitted and sliced thinly

2 red bell peppers

2 zucchinis, quartered

½ cup vegetable oil

½ cup olive oil

½ cup fresh lime juice

1 cup cilantro

1 cup parsley

1 jalapeno chili, seeded

2 cloves garlic

2 medium chipotle chilies, chopped finely

Dash of salt

Dash of pepper

Preparation:

- Put parsley, cilantro, garlic, jalapeno, olive oil, lime juice and salt in a food processor. Process all ingredients until well combined.

- Transfer the mixture to a bowl and add the chipotle chilies to it. Mix them well and set aside.

- Rub the steak and zucchini with olive oil. Season them with salt and pepper and let them stand for about 10 minutes.

- Grill the steak for about 4 minutes per side. Transfer it to a plate and cover loosely with aluminum foil for about 5 minutes.

- When cooled, slice it into thin strips and set aside.

- Grill the zucchini slices for about 4 minutes. Set aside to cool.

- Grill the red bell peppers for 10 minutes. Set aside to cool.

- Slice the zucchini further into diagonal slices and put them in a large bowl.

- Peel the bell peppers, remove their seeds and then dice them. Put them in the bowl too.

- Add the lettuce, radishes and avocado slices to the bowl.

- Pour the dressing over the salad and gently toss to combine.

- Top the salad with sliced steak and serve.

- This makes 4 servings.

Beef BBQ Wrap

Ingredients:

500 grams ground beef

3 teaspoons BBQ sauce

1 ripe avocado

1 tablespoon olive oil

1 onion, chopped

1 tablespoon tomato paste

2 medium tomatoes, sliced thinly

½ cup beef stock

1 head Boston lettuce, shredded

8 low-carb tortillas

Dash of salt

Dash of pepper

Preparation:

- Peel the avocado, remove stone, slice thinly and then set aside.

- In a pan, heat olive oil and fry the ground beef for about 3 minutes.

- Add the onion to the pan and continue to cook for another 5 minutes or until meat is browned.

- Add barbecue sauce to the mixture. Season it with salt and pepper.

- Add the beef stock and the tomato paste to the pan. Stir well to combine.

- Bring the mixture to a boil and then let it simmer for about 3 minutes or until sauce thickens.

- Lay a tortilla on a flat surface and put some beef mixture.

- Top with tomato slices, avocado slices and lettuce.

- Fold the tortilla into a wrap; continue to wrap the remaining ingredients.

- This makes 4 servings.

Dishes with Pork

Pork Cabbage Roll

Ingredients:

500 grams ground pork

1 medium carrot, shredded

1 head green cabbage

4 scallions, sliced thinly

½ cup chicken stock

2 tablespoons tomato paste

½ teaspoon dried sage

2 tablespoons apricot preserve

Dash of salt

Dash of pepper

Preparation:

- Put 2 cups of water into a pot and bring it to a boil.

- Put the cabbage leaves into the water and cook for about 6 minutes or until pliable.

- Remove the cabbage leaves from the pot and let them cool. Remove the thick core from each leaf.

- In a bowl, combine ground pork, tomato paste, carrot shreds, apricot preserve and chickens stock.

- Season the mixture with salt and pepper.

- Lay a cabbage leaf on a flat surface and place some of the pork mixture.

- Fold and roll the leaf. Place the roll on a steamer, seam side down.

- Continue to make rolls with the remaining ingredients.

- Steam the rolls for about 15 minutes.

- Let them cool and serve.

- This makes 4 servings.

Spicy Pork Coleslaw

Ingredients:

4 pork chops

1 red chili, chopped finely

3 cloves garlic, minced

1 green bell pepper

3 green onions, sliced thinly

1 tablespoon olive oil

2 tablespoons barbecue sauce

2 tablespoons mayonnaise

2 tablespoons sweetener

1 tablespoon white vinegar

½ cup light cream

2 medium carrots, peeled and shredded

4 cups cabbage, shredded

½ cup pecans, chopped

Preparation:

- In a bowl, combine barbecue sauce, garlic, chili and sweetener.
- Add the pork chops to the bowl and evenly coat them with the marinade.

- Cover the bowl and put it in the refrigerator for about 1 hour.

- Heat the olive oil in a pan and cook the pork for about 5 minutes per side.

- Let them cool and set aside.

- In a large bowl, combine shredded cabbage, shredded carrots and green bell pepper.

- Add the mayonnaise, pecans and the cream to the bowl and gently toss to combine.

- Serve the coleslaw with the pork.

- This makes 4 servings.

Cheesy Pork Burgers

Ingredients:

500 grams ground pork

1 clove garlic, minced

1 small onion, chopped

½ cup green chili peppers, chopped

3 medium tomatoes

4 slices bacon

¼ teaspoon dried sage 2 cups baby spinach

½ cup grated cheddar cheese

½ cup cream cheese

1 teaspoon white vinegar

Dash of salt

Dash of pepper

Preparation:

- In a bowl, combine tomatoes, green chili peppers and onion. Drain any liquid.

- Add salt and vinegar to the mixture and process them in the food processor until smooth. Set the mixture aside.

- Put the garlic and bacon in a food processor and process until the mixture reaches a coarsely ground texture.

- In a bowl, combine pork, sage and bacon mixture. Season it with salt and pepper.

- Form the mixture into four patties and refrigerate them for about 1 hour.

- Heat some oil in a pan and fry the patties for about 5 minutes.

- Flip the patties and continue to cook for another five minutes.

- When burgers are almost done, spread cheddar cheese and cream cheese on top of them.

- Reduce the heat, cover the pan and let the cheese melts.

- In a plate, place the baby spinach. Put the burgers on top of the spinach.

- Drizzle salsa on top of the burgers and serve.

- This makes 4 servings.

Spicy Pork Lettuce Wrap

Ingredients:

500 grams ground pork

1 cup water chestnut, diced

2 cloves garlic, minced

1 red bell pepper, diced finely

1 tablespoon sweet chili sauce

1 tablespoon fish sauce

2 scallions, sliced thinly

1 teaspoon ginger, grated

1 tablespoon canola oil

1 teaspoon sesame oil

2 tablespoons soy sauce

2 tablespoons cilantro, chopped

8 Boston lettuce leaves

Preparation:

- In a bowl, combine ground pork, sweet chili sauce, sesame oil, fish sauce, garlic, ginger and bell pepper.

- In a large pan, heat the canola oil.

- Add the pork mixture to the pan and cook for about 8 minutes.

- Stir constantly until the meat is slightly browned.

- Add the water chestnuts, soy sauce, cilantro and scallions to the pan.

- Stir well and remove the pan from heat. Let the pork mixture cool.

- Lay a lettuce leaf on a flat surface and put some pork mixture on it.

- Fold the leaf into a wrap and put it in a plate with the seam side down.

- Continue to wrap the remaining ingredients.

- This makes 4 servings.

Easy BBQ Meatballs

Ingredients:

500 grams ground pork

2 cups red cabbage, shredded

2 cups green cabbage, shredded

1 egg

¼ cup almond flour

1 teaspoon sweetener

¼ teaspoon cayenne pepper

1 teaspoon paprika

½ teaspoon ground cumin

1 tablespoon water

½ teaspoon salt

¼ teaspoon pepper

1 tablespoon dried onion flakes

2 teaspoons hot sauce

¼ cup yellow mustard

2 tablespoons vinegar

3 tablespoons sweetener

2 tablespoons ketchup

Dash of salt

Dash of pepper

Preparation:

- Put the mustard, hot sauce, onion flakes, sweetener, vinegar and ketchup on a pan. Stir well to combine.

- Season the mixture with salt and pepper and simmer for about 10 minutes.

- Remove the pan from heat and let the sauce cool.

- In a bowl, combine the ground pork, sweetener, paprika, cayenne pepper, cumin, egg, almond flour and water.

- Form the mixture into balls and ready them for frying.

- Heat some vegetable oil in a pan and fry the meatballs for about 5 minutes or until golden brown.

- Transfer the meatballs in paper towels to absorb excess oil.

- Cook in batches to avoid overcrowding the pan.

- In a separate bowl, whisk together the olive oil and the lemon juice.

- Season it with salt and pepper. Set it aside.

- In a large bowl, combine the red and green cabbage. Pour the dressing over the vegetables and gently toss t combine.

- Serve the meatballs with the cabbage slaw.

- This makes 4 servings.

Pork Berry Salad

Ingredients:

500 grams pork tenderloin

4 cups romaine lettuce, torn into bite-size pieces

2 cups fresh strawberries, halved

½ cup celery, sliced thinly

2 cloves garlic, minced

1 teaspoon fresh chives

2 tablespoons vegetable oil

¼ cup balsamic vinegar

¼ cup sweetener

¼ teaspoon pepper

2 tablespoons toasted walnuts, chopped

Dash of salt

Dash of pepper

Preparations:

- Slice the pork into thin slices, put them in a bowl and season them with salt and pepper.

- Heat some vegetable oil in a pan and cook the pork for about 10 minutes or until cooked through.

- Transfer the pork to a bowl and set aside.

- In the same pan, sauté the garlic. Add the sweetener, pepper and vinegar to the pan.

- Stir the mixture and cook for about 2 minutes. Set the dressing aside.

- Put the pork, romaine lettuce and strawberries in a large bowl.

- Pour the dressing over the salad and gently toss to combine.

- Top the salad with chopped walnuts and then serve.

- This makes 4 servings.

Chapter 4: Easy Recipes for Poultry

Dishes with Chicken

Grilled Chicken Tortilla

Ingredients:

4 boneless chicken breasts

¼ cup olive oil

¼ cup fresh lemon juice

1 tablespoon fresh lemon juice

1 teaspoon lemon zest

2 tablespoons garlic, minced

1 tablespoon Dijon mustard

1 cup sour cream

2 tablespoons Parmesan cheese, grated

1 teaspoon anchovy paste

4 low-carb tortillas

2 cups romaine lettuce, torn into bite-size pieces

2 cups cherry tomatoes, halved

Dash of salt

Dash of pepper

Preparation:

- In a bowl, whisk together 1 tablespoon garlic, lemon juice, lemon zest and olive oil.

- Add the chicken breasts to the bowl and toss to coat.

- Cover the bowl with plastic wrap and put it in the refrigerator overnight.

- Preheat the grill. Remove the chicken breasts from the marinade and pat them dry.

- Season the chicken breasts with salt and pepper and then grill them for about 12 minutes per side.

- Let the chicken breasts cool, slice them thinly and then set aside.

- In a separate bowl, mix 1 tablespoon lemon juice, mustard, garlic, anchovy paste, Parmesan cheese and sour cream. Season it with salt and pepper.

- Add the chicken slices, cherry tomatoes and romaine lettuce to the bowl.

- Gently toss to combine all the ingredients.

- Lay a tortilla on a flat surface and fill it with some of the chicken mixture.

- Fold the tortilla into a wrap. Continue wrapping the remaining ingredients.

- This makes 4 servings.

Chicken Apple Wrap

Ingredients:

4 chicken breasts, cooked

1 apple

2 teaspoons curry powder

2 tablespoons sour cream

2 tablespoons mayonnaise

2 teaspoons sweetener

1 rib celery

1 teaspoon ground ginger

¼ cup walnuts, chopped

8 lettuce leaves

Preparation:

- Cut the chicken into small cubes and then set aside.

- In a bowl, combine sour cream, mayonnaise, sweetener, ginger and curry powder and then set aside.

- Rinse the apple, pat it dry and cut it into small cubes. Put the cubes in a large bowl.

- Rinse the celery rib and then slice it very thinly. Add the celery slices to the large bowl.

- Add the sour cream mixture and the chopped walnuts to the bowl.

- Gently toss all the ingredients to combine.

- Lay a lettuce leaf on a flat surface and then put some of the chicken mixture on it.

- Fold the lettuce leaf into a wrap. Continue to wrap the remaining ingredients.

- This makes 4 servings.

Grilled Chicken Salad

Ingredients:

4 chicken breasts

1 hard boiled egg, chopped

1 cup cabbage, shredded

¼ cup cauliflower florets

1 cup butter lettuce, shredded

1 stalk celery, chopped

1 small cucumber, chopped

1 cup cherry tomatoes, halved

1 cup mushrooms, cooked and sliced

1 small zucchini, chopped

2 teaspoons heavy cream

¼ cup mayonnaise

2 teaspoons water

¼ teaspoon dried tarragon

¼ teaspoon fresh rosemary, chopped

½ cup blue cheese, crumbled

Dash of salt

Dash of pepper

Preparation:

- Season the chicken breasts with salt and pepper and let them stand for about 5 minutes.

- Set the grill on medium-high heat and grill the chicken breasts for about 5 minutes per side or until cooked through.

- Transfer them to a plate and set aside.

- In bowl, whisk together heavy cream, mayonnaise, rosemary, water, tarragon and blue cheese.

- Season the mixture with salt and pepper and then set aside.

- In a large bowl, combine cabbage, lettuce, celery, mushrooms, cauliflower, cucumber, egg, tomatoes and zucchini.

- Pour the dressing over the vegetables and gently toss to combine.

- Serve grilled chicken with salad.

- This makes 4 servings.

Chicken Lettuce Wrap

Ingredients:

500 grams chicken breasts, cubed

1 green onion, sliced thinly

1 teaspoon ginger, grated

½ teaspoon garlic powder

¼ teaspoon red pepper flakes

1 cup water chestnut, diced

1 cup carrot, shredded

½ cup mushrooms, chopped

½ cup almond, toasted and slivered

1 tablespoon soy sauce

2 tablespoons teriyaki sauce

2 tablespoons olive oil

8 Boston lettuce leaves

Preparation:

- Heat 1 tablespoon olive oil in a pan, add the chicken cubes to the pan and cook for 3 minutes or until chicken is cooked through.

- Add mushrooms, chestnuts, ginger and water to the pan and then continue to cook for another three minutes.

- In a large bowl, whisk together the remaining oil, soy sauce, teriyaki sauce, garlic powder, vinegar and red pepper flakes.

- Add the shredded carrots, almonds and cooked chicken to the bowl.

- Gently toss all the ingredients to combine.

- Lay a lettuce leaf on a flat surface and put some chicken mixture on it.

- Fold the leaf into a wrap and put it on plate seam side down.

- Continue to wrap the remaining ingredients.

- This makes 4 servings.

Stir-Fried Chicken

Ingredients:

4 chicken breasts

1 onion, chopped

1 teaspoon grated ginger

1 cup broccoli florets

1 medium carrot

2 cups mushrooms, sliced

1 bunch asparagus

1 egg

¼ teaspoon cayenne pepper

¼ cup chicken stock

1 tablespoon olive oil

Preparation:

- Peel the carrot, slice it into strips and then set aside.

- Rinse the asparagus, pat them dry, trim the bottom parts and then set aside.

- In a pan, heat olive oil and sauté onion for about 3 minutes.

- Cut the chicken breasts into strips and add them to the pan. Continue to cook for another three minutes.

- Add the chicken stock, asparagus, broccoli, ginger, mushrooms, carrot strips and cayenne pepper to the pan.

- Stir constantly until vegetables are tender. Season the mixture with salt and pepper.

- Scramble the egg and mix it with the vegetables.

- Serve immediately.

- This makes 4 servings.

BBQ Chicken Wrap

Ingredients:

4 chicken breasts

1 red bell pepper, diced

2 cloves garlic, chopped

2 scallions, chopped

1 orange, cut into wedges

1 teaspoon orange zest

1 cup chestnut, chopped

2 cups shiitake mushrooms

2 tablespoons vegetable oil

3 tablespoons barbecue sauce

1 head iceberg lettuce

Dash of salt

Dash of pepper

Preparation:

- Rinse mushrooms, pat them dry and remove tough stems.
- Slice mushrooms into thin strips and then set them aside.
- Slice the chicken breasts into thin strips and then set aside.

- In a pan, heat oil and add the chicken strips to it. Stir-fry the chicken strips for about 2 minutes.

- Add the mushrooms to the pan and continue to cook for another two minutes.

- Add ginger and garlic to the pan and then season the mixture with salt and pepper. Continue cooking for another minute.

- Add the water chestnut, bell pepper and orange zest to the pan. Continue to cook for another minute.

- Add the barbecue sauce to the pan and stir well to combine.

- Pile some lettuce leaves and put some chicken mixture on it.

- Fold the leaves into a wrap and serve it with orange wedges.

- Continue to wrap the remaining chicken mixture.

- This makes 4 servings.

Chicken Cheese Wrap

Ingredients:

4 boneless chicken breasts

1 shallot, minced

¼ teaspoon dried thyme leaves

4 tablespoons mayonnaise

2 teaspoons white vinegar

2 teaspoons Dijon mustard

4 slices cheddar cheese

2 cups baby spinach

4 low-carb tortillas

Dash of salt

Dash of pepper

Preparation:

- Place the chicken breasts in a pan and cover them with water.

- Season water with salt and pepper and bring it to a boil. Cook the chicken for about 10 minutes or until cooked through.

- Let the chicken breasts cool, slice them thinly crosswise and then set aside.

- In a large bowl, whisk together vinegar, Dijon mustard, thyme and shallot. Season the mixture with salt and pepper.

- Add the chicken slices to the bowl and gently toss to combine all ingredients.

- Lay a tortilla on a flat surface. Layer some spinach, a slice of cheese and a scoop of chicken mixture on it.

- Fold the tortilla into a wrap.

- Continue to wrap the rest of the ingredients.

- This makes 4 servings.

Chicken Curry Wrap

Ingredients:

4 boneless chicken breasts

2 cloves garlic, minced

1 jalapeno, sliced thinly

2 scallions, sliced thinly

1 lemon, halved

3 tablespoons cilantro, chopped

3 sprigs cilantro

1 tablespoon mayonnaise

¼ sour cream

2 teaspoons curry powder

1 apple, pitted and sliced into bite-size chunks

¼ cup almonds, chopped

Preparation:

- Put the chicken breasts in deep pot and cover with water.
- Add cilantro sprigs, garlic, jalapeno and half of a lemon.
- Bring the water to a boil and then simmer for about 15 minutes.
- Use a slotted spoon and transfer the chicken breasts in a plate. Cover the

plate with aluminum foil and let stand for about 5 minutes.

- When the chicken breasts are cool enough, cut them into bite-size cubes and set aside.

- In a bowl, mix sour cream, mayonnaise, lemon juice, scallions, chopped cilantro, apple, almonds and curry powder. Season the mixture with salt and pepper.

- Add the chicken cubes to the bowl and toss to coat.

- Lay a lettuce leaf on a flat surface and put some of the chicken mixture on it.

- Fold the leaf into a wrap. Continue to wrap the remaining chicken mixture.

- This makes 4 servings.

Dishes with Turkey

Turkey Burger Salad

Ingredients:

500 grams ground turkey

½ cup olive oil

¼ cup red wine vinegar

1 teaspoon fresh thyme

2 cloves garlic

1 teaspoon fresh parsley

1 teaspoon fresh oregano

1 medium zucchini, chopped

2 cups baby spinach

2 tomatoes, chopped

Dash of salt

Dash of pepper

Preparation:

- Put the garlic, oregano, parsley, thyme, vinegar, salt and pepper in a blender.

- Blend the ingredients and slowly add the olive oil until well combined. Set the mixture aside.

- In a bowl, combine ground turkey, salt and pepper.

- Form the mixture into 4 patties. Set them aside.

- Heat olive oil in a pan and fry the patties for about five minutes per side or until they are cooked through.

- Transfer them on paper towels to absorb excess oil.

- In a large bowl, combine spinach, zucchini and tomatoes.

- Pour the dressing over the salad and gently toss to combine.

- Arrange some salad in a plate, top with turkey burger and then serve.

- This makes 4 servings.

Grilled Turkey Burger

Ingredients:

500 grams ground turkey

2 cups romaine lettuce, torn into bite-size pieces

1 avocado, peeled, pitted and sliced thinly

2 tomatoes, sliced thinly

4 slices cheddar cheese

1 teaspoon salt

1 teaspoon pepper

Preparation:

- In a bowl, combine ground turkey, salt and pepper.

- Form the mixture into patties and grill them over medium heat for about 5 minutes per side.

- Top each burger patty with a slice of cheddar cheese. Let the cheese melt before removing burgers from heat.

- Serve burgers over a bed of lettuce.

- This makes 4 servings.

Turkey Meatballs

Ingredients:

500 grams ground turkey

1 onion, chopped

1 egg, beaten

1 teaspoon ground cumin

½ cup salsa

½ cup almond flour

¼ cup heavy cream

5 tablespoons canola oil

4 ounce feta cheese, cut into small cubes

½ cup chicken stock

¼ cup water

1 teaspoon salt

½ teaspoon pepper

Preparation:

- In a pan, heat 1 tablespoon canola oil and sauté onion for about 5 minutes and then set aside.

- In a large bowl, combine turkey, cumin, onion, garlic, egg, salt and pepper.

- Form the mixture into balls. Insert cheese into the center of each ball.

- Heat the remaining oil in the pan and cook the balls for about 5 minutes or until all sides are golden brown.

- Add chicken stock and salsa to the pan. Cover the pan and simmer for about 10 minutes.

- Transfer the meatballs and sauce in a serving dish.

- This makes 4 servings.

Turkey Roast Salad

Ingredients:

500 grams turkey

1 clove garlic, minced

1 onion, chopped

1 tablespoon tarragon leaves, chopped

2 stalks celery, chopped

1 tablespoon chives, chopped

¼ teaspoon cayenne pepper

2 tablespoons parsley, chopped

2 cups mixed greens

3 tablespoons fresh lemon juice

¼ cup almonds, chopped

3 tablespoons olive oil

½ cup sour cream

¼ cup mayonnaise

1 tablespoon sweetener

Dash of salt

Dash of pepper

Preparation:

- In a bowl, whisk together mayonnaise, sour cream, sweetener and olive oil.

- Season it with salt and pepper and then set aside.

- Put the turkey in a bowl. Add cayenne pepper, lemon juice and garlic to the bowl.

- Season the turkey with slat and pepper and then toss to coat.

- Transfer the turkey to a baking pan line with aluminum foil.

- Put the baking pan in the oven and bake at 200 °F for about 20 minutes or until golden.

- Remove the baking pan from the oven. Let the turkey cool and then pull the meat into strips.

- In a large bowl, combine turkey, celery, onion and almonds.

- Pour the dressing over the salad and gently toss to combine.

- Serve turkey salad on a bed of mixed greens.

- This makes 4 servings.

Chapter 5: Easy Recipes with Seafood

Dishes with Fish

Tuna Lettuce Boat

Ingredients:

2 cups tuna flakes

1 stalk celery, sliced thinly

1 teaspoon parsley, minced

1 small red onion, minced

1 tablespoon Dijon mustard

1 tablespoon fresh lemon juice

½ cup mayonnaise

4 hard-boiled eggs, sliced into wedges

8 butter lettuce leaves

Dash of salt

Dash of pepper

Preparation:

- In a bowl, combine tuna flakes, parsley, onion and celery.

- Add mustard, lemon juice and mayonnaise to the tuna mixture.

- Season the mixture with salt and pepper and stir to combine.

- Lay the lettuce leaves and put some tuna mixture on the center.

- Top with boiled egg wedges and serve immediately.

- This makes 4 servings.

Fruity Tuna Tortilla

Ingredients:

500 grams tuna steak

1 hard-boiled egg

2 tablespoons green onion, minced

1 teaspoon lemon juice

¼ cup raisins

1 cup pineapple tidbits

¼ cup celery, diced

1 teaspoon Dijon mustard

3 tablespoons mayonnaise

2 medium tomatoes, sliced thinly

1 cup romaine lettuce, torn into bite-size pieces

8 low-carb tortillas

Dash of salt

Dash of pepper

Preparation:

- Season the tuna steak with salt and pepper. Sprinkle the lemon juice over the tuna steak and let it stand for about 8 minutes.

- Preheat the grill and cook tuna steak over medium-high heat for about 4 minutes per side.

- Let the tuna steak cool, chop it coarsely and then set aside.

- Slice the egg into half, remove the yolk and set aside.

- Dice the egg whites and set aside.

- In a large bowl, combine diced egg whites, raisins, green onion, mustard, mayonnaise, pineapple and tuna.

- Lay a tortilla on a flat surface and put some lettuce on the center.

- Put some tuna mixture on the bed of lettuce and top with tomato slices.

- Fold the tortilla into a wrap. Continue to wrap the remaining ingredients.

- This makes 4 servings.

Easy Tuna Salad

Ingredients:

2 cups tuna flakes

1 cup green grapes, halved

1 cup red grapes, halved

½ cup kalamata olives

1 green bell pepper

2 tablespoons fresh oregano, chopped

1 red onion, sliced thinly

1 cucumber

1 head butter lettuce, torn into bite-size pieces

¼ cup apple cider vinegar

3 tablespoons olive oil

½ cup feta cheese, crumbled

Preparation:

- Peel the cucumber, slice it into small cubes and then set aside.

- Cut the green bell pepper into half, remove the seeds, slice it into small cubes and then set aside.

- In a large bowl, combine lettuce, onion, tomatoes, kalamata olives, bell pepper, oregano and tuna.

- In a separate bowl, whisk together olive oil and vinegar. Season it with salt and pepper.

- Pour the dressing over the salad and gently toss to combine.

- Serve immediately.

- This makes 4 servings.

Salmon Wrap

Ingredients:

8 slices smoked salmon

1 red onion, minced

6 hard-boiled eggs

6 tablespoons Dijon mustard

1 cup mayonnaise

2 cups baby spinach

8 low-carb tortilla

Preparation:

- In a small bowl, whisk together mayonnaise, Dijon mustard and minced onion. Set the mixture aside.

- Peel the eggs, slice them thinly and then set aside.

- Lay a tortilla on a flat surface and spread some dressing on it.

- Put some spinach, egg and salmon on it.

- Roll up the tortilla tightly. Continue to wrap the remaining ingredients.

- This makes 4 servings.

Salmon Herb Salad

Ingredients:

200 grams salmon fillet

¼ cup fresh lemon juice

1 tablespoon sweetener

2 tablespoons fresh dill, chopped

¼ cup kalamata olives

1 red onion, chopped

2 red bell peppers, chopped

1 tablespoon olive oil

1 small cucumber, chopped

2 cups mixed greens

Dash of salt

Dash of pepper

Preparation;

- In a bowl, whisk together lemon juice, sweetener, dill and olive oil. Season it with salt and pepper and then set aside.

- Pat the salmon fillet dry and drizzle olive oil on it. Season it with salt and pepper and gently rub to coat.

- Line a baking pan with aluminum foil and place the salmon in it.

- Put the baking pan in the oven and roast at 425 °F for about 6 minutes.

- Let the salmon cool, flake it with a fork and then set aside.

- In a large bowl, combine salad greens, bell pepper, cucumber, red onion and kalamata olives.

- Pour the dressing over the salad and gently toss to combine.

- Serve immediately.

- This makes 4 servings.

Dishes with Shrimp and Scallop

Spicy Shrimp Salad

Ingredients:

500 grams shrimp, peeled and deveined

2 cups alfalfa sprouts

1 shallot, chopped

½ teaspoon coriander

½ teaspoon paprika

¼ cup white vinegar

½ cup water

½ teaspoon red pepper flakes

1 tablespoon olive oil

1 cup cooked white beans

2 tablespoons parley, chopped

Dash of salt

Dash of pepper

Preparation:

- In a large pan, heat the olive oil and add the shrimps to it.

- Add paprika, shallot, coriander, red pepper flakes, dash of salt and pepper to the pan. Stir and cook for about 5 minutes or until shrimps are pink and opaque.

- Transfer the shrimps to a plate and set aside.

- In the same pan, put the beans, water and vinegar. Cook the beans for about 5 minutes.

- Drain the liquid and transfer beans to a bowl. Let the beans cool.

- In a large bowl, combine the alfalfa sprouts, shrimps and beans.

- Top with chopped parley and then serve immediately.

- This makes 4 servings.

Coco Shrimp Cakes

Ingredients:

500 grams shrimp, peeled and deveined

1 tablespoon chives, chopped

¼ cup coconut flakes

1 egg, beaten

½ cup mayonnaise

3 tablespoons vegetable oil

2 tablespoons olive oil

1 tablespoon white vinegar

4 radishes

1 cup cherry tomatoes, quartered

4 cups mixed greens

Dash of salt

Dash of pepper

Preparation:

- Chop the shrimps coarsely and put them in a bowl.

- Add beaten egg, coconut flakes, chives and mayonnaise to the bowl.

- Toss the ingredients to combine. Season the mixture with salt and pepper.

- Cover the bowl with plastic wrap and put it in the refrigerator for about 1 hour.

- Form the shrimp mixture into patties.

- In a pan, heat vegetable olive oil and fry the shrimp patties for about 4 minutes per side.

- Fry in batches to avoid overcrowding the pan.

- Transfer the shrimp cakes on paper towels to absorb excess oil.

- In a large bowl, whisk together the olive oil and vinegar. Season it with salt and pepper.

- Add the shrimp cakes, tomatoes, radishes and mixed greens to the bowl. Toss to combine.

- Serve immediately.

- This makes 4 servings.

Shrimp Lettuce Wrap

Ingredients:

500 grams shrimp, peeled and deveined

2 teaspoons fish sauce

2 cloves garlic, minced

¼ cup fresh mint, chopped

2 tablespoons vegetable oil

¼ cup cashew nuts, chopped

1 ripe mango

8 Boston lettuce leaves

Preparation:

- Chop the shrimps coarsely and set aside.

- In a large pan, heat the vegetable oil and sauté garlic for about 2 minutes.

- Add the shrimps and the fish sauce to the pan; stir to combine.

- Season it with salt and pepper and cook for about 5 minutes or until shrimps are pink and opaque.

- Peel the mango and remove the stone. Slice the mango into thin strips.

- Lay a lettuce leaf on a flat surface. Put some shrimp mixture, mango slices, some mint and chopped cashews.

- Fold the leaf into a wrap. Continue to wrap the remaining ingredients.

- This makes 4 servings.

Shrimp Herb Salad

Ingredients:

500 grams shrimp, peeled and deveined

6 tablespoons fresh dill, minced

3 stalks celery, minced

1 red onion, minced

1 cup red cabbage, shredded

1 cup green cabbage, shredded

1 lemon, quartered

1 teaspoon Dijon mustard

2 tablespoons white vinegar

2 cups mayonnaise

Dash of salt

Dash of pepper

Preparation:

- Put the shrimps in pan and cover them with water.

- Add the lemon quarters to the pan. Season it with salt and pepper.

- Bring the water to a boil and cook for 5 minutes or until shrimps are pink and opaque.

- Drain liquid and let the shrimps cool.

- In a large bowl, whisk together mustard, mayonnaise, vinegar and dill. Season the mixture with salt and pepper.

- Add the green cabbage, red cabbage, celery, onion and shrimps to the bowl and then toss to combine.

- Chill the salad before serving.

- This makes 4 servings.

Seared Scallops

Ingredients:

500 grams scallop

2 cups sugar snap peas

3 teaspoons canola oil

12 slices bacon

Dash of salt

Dash of pepper

Preparation:

- Rinse the sugar snap peas and pat them dry. Trim the end and slice them diagonally.

- In a pan, heat 1 teaspoon canola oil and cook the sugar snap peas for about 2 minutes.

- Season them with salt and pepper. Transfer them to a bowl and let them cool.

- In the same pan, cook the bacon for about 3 minutes per side or until crisp.

- Transfer the bacon on paper towels to absorb excess oil. Chop the bacon coarsely.

- In the same pan, sauté shallots for about minute. Transfer the sautéed shallots to a bowl to cool.

- Sprinkle salt and pepper on scallops.

- In the same pan, heat the remaining canola oil and cook scallops for about 2 minutes per side.

- Cook in batches if necessary to avoid overcrowding the pan.

- In a bowl, combine sugar snap peas, shallots and bacon.

- Top the mixture with scallops and serve.

- This makes 4 servings.

Fruity Scallop Salad

Ingredients:

500 grams scallop

2 tablespoons butter, melted

¼ cup olive oil

6 tablespoons fresh lime juice

2 green onions, sliced thinly

1 jalapeno chili, seeded and minced

1 avocado

1 ripe mango

4 cups mixed greens

Dash of salt

Dash of pepper

Preparation:

- In a small bowl, whisk together lime juice, olive oil and jalapeno chili.

- Season it with salt and pepper and then set aside.

- Peel the mango, remove the stone, slice it into small cubes and set aside.

- Cut the avocado into half, remove the stone and slice it into small cubes. Put the cubes in the bowl with the mango cubes.

- Pour 3 tablespoons lime juice over the fruit mixture, toss to coat and then set aside.

- Put the scallops in a bowl and pour the remaining lime juice over them. Toss to coat them evenly.

- Prepare a baking tray lined with aluminum foil.

- Arrange the scallops on the baking tray in a single layer.

- Put the baking tray in broiler and broil for about 4 minutes or until scallops are opaque and golden.

- In a large bowl, combine salad greens, mango, avocado and scallops.

- Pour the dressing over the salad and gently toss to combine.

- Serve immediately.

- This makes 4 servings.

Easy Shrimp Tortilla

Ingredients:

500 grams shrimp, peeled and deveined

2 tablespoons garlic, minced

3 tablespoons fresh lemon juice

1 tablespoon barbecue sauce

2 tablespoons butter

2 chipotle chilies, mashed

1 cup Gouda cheese, shredded

8 low-carb tortilla

Dash of salt

Dash of pepper

Preparation:

- In a large pan, melt the butter and sauté garlic for about 2 minutes.

- Add the shrimps to the pan and season them with salt and pepper. Cook for about 4 minutes or until shrimps are pink and cooked through.

- Pour the lemon juice over the shrimps. Stir well and then set aside.

- In a bowl, combine chipotle paste and barbecue sauce then set aside.

- Lay a tortilla on a flat surface and spread some chipotle paste on it.

- Place some shrimps and some Gouda cheese on top of the chipotle paste.

- Fold the tortilla into a wrap. Continue to wrap the remaining ingredients.

- This makes 4 servings.

Sweet Spicy Shrimp Salad

Ingredients:

500 grams shrimp, peeled and deveined

1 shallot, chopped finely

½ teaspoon red pepper flakes

¼ cup olive oil

1 tablespoon mustard

2 tablespoons apple cider vinegar

1 tablespoon sweetener

2 cups baby spinach

½ cup feta cheese, crumbled

Dash of salt

Dash of pepper

Preparation:

- In a pan, heat vegetable oil and fry shrimps for about 3 minutes or until they are pink and opaque.

- Put the shrimps in a bowl and let them cool.

- In a bowl, whisk together olive oil, vinegar, sweetener, shallot and red pepper flakes. Season it with salt and pepper.

- In large bowl, combine spinach and shrimps. Pour the dressing over the salad and toss to combine.

- Top salad with crumbled feta cheese and serve.

- This makes 4 servings.

Conclusion

Thank you again for purchasing this book!

I hope this book was able to help you to find better and easier ways to prepare lunch that adheres to Atkins Diet.

The next step is to make sure that you apply all the things that you have learned from this book in your daily food preparation.

Thank you and good luck!